EXPLORING HISTORIC CUMBRIA

Over 300 Places to Visit

Researched & Written by Richard Catlow

Photographs by Stuart Mason

Published by Countryside Publications, School Lane, Brinscall, Chorley, Lancashire

Printed by Tamley-Reed Limited

Text © Richard Catlow, 1978

Photographs © Stuart Mason, 1978

ISBN 0 86157 005 7

Chapter · Contents · Page

Chapter	Contents	Page
1	Bedrock of History	4
2	Around Ambleside	5
3	Around Hawkshead	6
4	Around Keswick	7
5	Around Cockermouth	9
6	Around Ullswater	10
7	West of the Lakes	11
8	Furness & Cartmel	14
9	Around Kendal	19
10	Kirkby Lonsdale	23
11	Penrith & the Vale of Eden	24
12	Carlisle, Solway & the Border	30
13	The Coal Towns	39
14	Wordsworth & the Poets	41
15	Hadrian's Wall	46
*	**24 Pages of Illustrations**	*

1   Bedrock of History

Cumbria's history is in many ways an extension of its geography. For it was Cumbria's mountains and rivers, its fertile valleys and mineral rich hills and, perhaps above all, its closeness to the Scottish border, that have shaped the story of this beautiful part of England.

The Lakeland mountains provided refuge for defeated Britons after the fall of Rome. In fact it was these "Cymru", as they called themselves, that gave Cumbria its name. The Mountains also made a home for Vikings from the fijords of Norway and it is their words, like thwaite, gill, tarn, beck and fell, which dominate the map today. They abandoned their fierce pagan gods and built a great cross to their new, much gentler religion, at Gosforth, and smaller crosses elsewhere. Their hog back graves of carved stone – little houses for the souls of the dead – are still to be found in many Cumbrian churches. Cumbria was also part of the Anglo-Saxon Kingdom of Northumbria, which, for a few brief years, was the flower of European civilisation. A fragment of that glory remains at Bewcastle, in a cross of unsurpassed beauty. The proximity of Scotland – and Cumbria was even part of Scotland for some years after the Norman Conquest – taught generations of Cumbrians to keep a wary eye to the north.

But the first people to defend the region were the Romans, with their great wall running from the Solway to the east coast. The Norman lords, and that included some fighting bishops and monks practising their own version of muscular Christianity, built castles to dominate strategic points like river crossings.

Lesser lords and better-off yeomen built their own, smaller versions of these castles. These, Pele towers as they are called, were a place of refuge during the frequent Scottish raids. Many of them still survive, ranging from imposing structures to farmhouses or churches with thick walls, slit windows and a few battlements. It was only after the union of the two kingdoms that Cumbrians could relax, though there was a later Scottish invasion – to work the pits that grew up around Workington and Whitehaven.

Elsewhere Lakeland green slates were being worked to keep

homes dry, copper was mined and Borrowdale "wadd" gave rise to a pencil industry at Keswick. In the south the Furness district could have been rechristened "Furnace", as iron ore was worked and foundries sprang up.

Cumbria's towns and villages are built of stones of every hue: sandstone the angry red of a weatherbeaten face or as pale pink as a maiden's blush, limestone glistening white in the sun and the darker hues of slate and volcanic stone.

If you'd asked anyone in the early 17th century what they thought of the Lake District, words like "dismal", "drear" and "forbidding" would have been used. It was people like Wordsworth, Coleridge and Ruskin who taught us to recognise the beauty of the Lakeland scene. But, even in their wildest dreams, they could have hardly foreseen their success. Wealthy Victorians built Italianate villas on the shores of Windermere. The less wealthy came on rail excursions and enjoyed boat trips on the lake.

Gradually the whole of Lakeland was opened up, until today people come in their millions and the National Park Authority, the National Trust and other bodies have to try their best to make sure that original spirit, which inspired the poets, is not lost.

2   Around Ambleside

Ambleside in the summer months is usually awash with tourists, but small alleyways lead off the main street to quieter spots. St Anne's Church has a memorial window to Wordsworth, who distributed postage stamps from an office in the town, but Ambleside's best known building is probably also its smallest. Bridge House, spanning a little river, was once a summer house set in orchards. Now it is a National Trust information centre.

Across the hill at Troutbeck, Town End is one of those typical, rambling old Lakeland farmsteads with thick walls and towering round chimney stacks. They were the home of a fiercely independent breed of farmer, known as statesmen. The Browne family once lived here, now it is owned by the National Trust.

The Mortal Man Inn has a distinctive inn sign painted in 1800 by a local painter with an even more distinctive name. He was Julius Caesar Ibbetson!

At Bowness the church of St Martin dates back to 1483. Inside is a German wood carving of the saint and a beggar. The east window has stained glass, possibly taken from Cartmel Priory or Furness Abbey. On Windermere itself, Belle Isle gets its name from the splendid mansion built on it in 1774 and having the distinction to be cylindrical. On the A591, east of Windermere town, is Ings, where the church of St Anne was built in Renaissance style by a local boy who went to London and amassed a vast fortune. This Westmorland Dick Whittington was called Robert Bateman. He built his church in 1743 and also built almshouses where old folk could see out their days in comfort. Inside the church is a memorial to Bateman with an epitaph by Wordsworth.

A quiet spot is Kentmere, at the head of beautiful Kentdale reached by a narrow road from Staveley on the A591. St Cuthbert's church has a splendid bronze memorial to Bernard Gilpin whose religious work gained him the title "The Apostle of the North". For centuries Gilpins lived at Kentmere Hall, a fine pele tower attached to a cottage.

3 *Around* Hawkshead

Hawkshead with its picturesque huddle of cottages set in a most charming landscape deserves to be known for many other things besides the residence of Wordsworth and Beatrix Potter here.

In the main square is the old meat market, the Shambles, which was built more than two centuries ago, and the Town Hall built in 1887. On the hill to the church you pass Pillar House, with a flight of stone steps supported by the columns which gave it its name.

The church of St Michael and All Angels dates mainly from 1350, though part is 200 years older. Inside, the Sandys Chapel was built by William and Mary Sandys, whose son, Edwin, became Archbishop of York. The archbishop founded Hawkshead Grammar School in 1675.

The church has more than 200 burial in woollen certificates recalling an Act of Parliament which sought to turn death to the benefit of Britain's wool industry by insisting on woollen shrouds One is on show by the north door. The church also has a mini-museum of old halberds from village processions, staffs of office, a pitch pipe for setting the key for psalms, and weights for the village market. At the east end of the church is a stone bench where sales took place and notices were read after services.

Thimble Hall, with its overhanging upper-storey, was given to the National Trust by Beatrix Potter.

All that remains of Hawkshead Hall is the gatehouse. The hall was built by the monks of Furness to oversee their lands in this area. In the 15th century it was their manorial court. Now the gatehouse shelters a National Trust folk museum. Over its doorway is a carving of a lion's head. There's also a fine, traceried window and a huge fireplace with dog tooth work.

Esthwaite Hall, on the west bank of Esthwaite Water, was the birthplace of Archbishop Sandys. Nearby Esthwaite Lodge, now a youth hostel, was once the home of novelist Francis Brett Young.

4   *c*Around Keswick

Keswick is famous not only for its scenery, but for its pencil industry, which grew up when graphite – or "wadd" as it is known locally – was discovered in Borrowdale. There is a museum of pencil making.

Keswick's most noticeable building is the whitewashed Moot Hall in the main street, restored in 1813 but dating from much earlier.

Keswick's historic church is dedicated to St Kentigern and stands just outside the town at Crosthwaite. It has a font, given by Lady Maude Percy in 1932 as a tribute to a former vicar, a 14th century window from Furness Abbey, a fine memorial of 1527 to Sir John Radcliffe, a sundial more than 350 years old and a set of old rhymes warning bell ringers about their behaviour. The church treasure is a set of twelve consecration crosses, representing the twelve apostles, and made when this historic building was founded.

From Keswick the energetic can row out to St Herbert's Isle on Derwentwater, where a small ruined chapel can be discovered among the dense undergrowth. It dates from the 14th century, but reminds us of a much older story.

It is dedicated to St Herbert, a Christian hermit whio lived here in Anglo-Saxon times to avoid distraction from his spiritual work. He was a friend of St Cuthbert and, when the two met at Carlisle, they prayed they should both die in the same hour. They did in 687. On St Herbert's Day, April 13th, mass used to be celebrated on the island.

In the lovely Newlands Valley, to the west of Derwentwater, is the farm of Stair, which bears the inscription "T.F. 1647". It is said Thomas Fairfax, commander of the Parliamentary forces in the Civil War, stayed here.

Just out of Keswick, off the A591, Ambleside road, is Lakeland's most famous prehistoric monument: Castlerigg Stone Circle. This great oval of standing stones, enclosing a group of smaller stones, is romantically set on a plateau surrounded by wild mountains. It was probably .Castlerigg that Keats had in mind when he wrote of a "dismal cirque of Druid stones upon a forlorn moor".

Nowadays we know better than Keats, even if we can't express ourselves so well. The stone circles had nothing to do with druids, or scenes of human sacrifice. They were the product of an advanced civilisation which used them to calculate the movement of the moon and other celestial bodies.

Above the road near Thirlmere is another ancient monument: Shoulthwaite Castle. This is a hill fort guarded by three great trenches, the remains of which can still be seen.

At Threlkeld, on the A66 east of Keswick, Threlkeld Hall nestles against the slopes of Blencathra. It was once the home of Sir Lancelot Threlkeld, who said he had one home for profit and warmth in winter, one home for pleasure and this one to provide him with tenants to fight with him in the wars. His stepson Henry Clifford escaped his enemies, the Yorkists, by living here as a shepherd lad.

5   ẞAround Cockermouth

Cockermouth is a pleasant, bustling market town at the heart of a gentle country just beyond the Lakeland mountains.

The castle, considerable parts of which remain, was once captured by Robert the Bruce on one of his border forays. Piers Gaveston, the favourite of King Edward II, was constable here. When the castle was damaged again in a later Scottish raid stones from Roman Papcastle, nearby, were used to repair it. Another famous person to come here was Mary Queen of Scots in 1586, at the beginning of her unfortunate time in England when she was forced to throw herself on the mercy of her cousin Elizabeth I. Good Queen Bess wasn't renowned for mercy and later Mary was executed. The castle, the home of lord Egremont, is open to the public when he is not in residence.

In the main street is an impressive statue of Lord Mayo, a former Cockermouth MP who became Viceroy of India.

At the back of the main street, beneath the castle mound, a lane leads through the yard of Jennings' brewery, where brewing is still an art not a science.

South of the A66, at Wythop, a ruined Tudor chapel can be reached by an attractive walk through the fields.

Isel, to the north-east of Cockermouth and reached by country lanes, stands by the River Derwent. The church of St Michael is a beautiful Norman building and a window has three sundials on it to mark monastic hours, for, before the Reformation, this was a chapel of Hexham Abbey. Also to be seen are two Anglo-Saxon stones carved with Christian symbols. Nearby is an ancient three-arched bridge.

Not far away is magnificent Isel Hall, once an old pele tower, which grew to become an Elizabethan mansion. It was once the home of Elizabeth Lawson, who loved and was loved by James Wolfe, the hero of Quebec.

Hewthwaite Hall, on the other bank of the Derwent, is another fine house, dating from 1581. An inscription over the doorway says it was built by John and Elizabeth Swynburn.

Bridekirk, to the north of the A595 Carlisle road, has two churches dedicated to St Bridget; a relatively new one and an ancient one in ruins. In the yard are Anglo-Saxon remains, but Bridekirk's chief glory is its font, covered with miraculous carvings and runic inscriptions which say this is the workmanship of Richard.

On the A595 at Mealsgate, Whitehall was once a great manor house. The original pele tower is all that now remains. It can be visited by appointment. Four miles south of Cockermouth, along the B5292 and B5289, is Lorton Hall, which can also be visited by appointment. It is an old pele tower with a Jacobean extension. The exiled King Charles II stayed here on a secret visit to Cumbria to rally support for his cause.

Eaglesfield, west of the A5086 Cockermouth–Egremont road, may only be a small place, but it has produced more famous people than many a town.

A house in the village is marked with a plaque to record that John Dalton was born here in 1766. A child prodigy, who became village schoolteacher at 12, he later formulated the atomic theory, which has been put into practice at Calder Hall, only a few miles away. The village church, called the John Dalton Memorial Church, was built by the Royal Society to commemorate him.

At Moorland Close, just off the A road to the north, was born a rather more notorious character: Fletcher Christian of Mutiny on the Bounty fame.

On a limestone crag at nearby Pardshaw, George Fox, the Quaker, preached one of his memorable sermons to an audience of more than 10,000 people.

6   Around Ullswater

Ullswater is famous for Wordsworth's daffodils and for the dramatic ridges soaring to the summit of Helvellyn.

Patterdale Hall, to the north of Patterdale village, was once the home of the Mounseys, who were proudly known as the "Kings of Patterdale".

Further down the lake side, where the A5091 and A592 part ways, stands Lyulph's Tower, a romantic folly built by the Duke of Norfolk in 1780.

At Martindale, on the opposite bank of the lake, St Martin's church, built in 1633, is a beautiful example of a simple Lakeland church.

7   West of the Lakes

The western Lake District has the wildest scenery, the highest mountains, the deepest lake and a narrow strip of lowland country bordering the sea that is rich in historical remains.

Ravenglass, sleepy fishing village on the shores of an "inland sea" created by the meeting of three river mouths, is at the centre of this area. The "inland sea" – it is linked to the sea proper by a narrow channel – has provided shelter for fishing craft and smugglers' boats, but probably its first users were Roman galleys which lay at rest here off the Roman fort of Clanoventa.

On the edge of the sea, just beyond the village, can be seen the mounds which mark almost all that is left of Roman Ravenglass. I say almost, because sheltered in a conifer plantation nearby – reached by path or lane from the village – is Walls Castle; the remains of the Roman bath house. Its walls, some 13 ft high, are said to be the highest Roman walls in the country. You can still see the original orange-red plaster with which they were lined and a niche which must have contained a bust or statue.

Ravenglass is the terminus of the Ravenglass and Eskdale Railway, now a popular tourist attraction, but originally built to carry iron ore. The "Lal Ratty", as it is affectionately known, was built by the Whitehaven Iron Mines Ltd in 1875. Originally of 3 ft gauge it was reopened as a 15 inch line by a model railway engineer earlier this century. There is a railway museum at Ravenglass station.

Another piece of working history, just off the A595 coast road and with its own station on the "Ratty", is Muncaster Mill; where the water wheel turns under the force of the mill race and the ponderous wooden machinery creaks gently as it turns. You can buy wholesome flour here, and in Ravenglass mention "John's Specials" at the bread shop to buy a loaf made from this.

St Michael's Church, Muncaster, at the entrance to the Muncaster Garden Centre, is a picturesque spot set amid trees. The remains of a Viking cross can be discovered in its grounds.   Muncaster Castle is the home of the Pennington family, who have been here a very long time. It has a superb position amid exotically landscaped gardens. The castle incorporates an old pele tower, but it was largely rebuilt in the last two centuries. The visitor will find much to admire, including the fine octagonal library lined with great volumes, the Elizabethan hall and the portrait of Thomas Skelton, the fool of Muncaster.

In 1464 a travel-weary stranger was discovered by shepherds on the neighbouring fellside. He turned out to be the fugitive King Henry VI, fleeing from defeat in battle. The Chapel's Monument marks the place the monarch was discovered. The tower on Newtown Knott, to the west of the castle, was built in 1823 to guide mariners.

A place of tranquil beauty is Hall Waberthwaite Church, reached by minor road from the A595 just south of Muncaster. The tiny church has an ancient cross in its yard.

South on the A595 is Bootle, which has an interesting old church with a brass memorial to Sir Hugh Askew, knighted by Edward VI at the Battle of Pinkie. To the north the remains of an ancient nunnery still exist among the farm buildings at Seaton Hall.

In scenic Eskdale the church of St Catherine at Boot is hidden away in a riverside meadow. It is a place full of charm and interest. In its yard is the tomb of noted Eskdale huntsman Tommy Dobson, with a portrait of fox and hounds. Nearby is ancient Dalegarth Hall, with great rounded chimneys. Eskdale Mill, at Boot is reached by a 17th century packhorse bridge. It dates back to 1578 and is now a museum.

At the head of Eskdale is Hardknott Fort, a partially reconstructed Roman fortress which must have one of the grandest settings of any of Rome's great works. It stands just off the Hardknott Pass, overlooked by towering mountains. Buildings beyond the protecting walls show that even in this wild place the tribes came to accept the rule of Rome.

The dale to the north of Eskdale is deep and desolate Wasdale. The church of Nether Wasdale at Strands village, was a chapel of St Bee's Priory and has oak panelling from York Minster.

The tiny church at Wasdale Head is set in the "climber's graveyard", where tombstones tell of tragedy on the surrounding fells. Also buried here is Will Ritson, landlord of the nearby hotel, who won a reputation as a notorious liar.

Back in the coastal lands, Irton church – reached by a minor road from the A595 north of Ravenglass – stands almost alone on a green hill. The church is undistinguished, but nearby stands the Iron Cross, 10 ft high and dating back 1,000 years. Almost every inch of its red sandstone surface is covered by intricate carvings.

North along the A595 is Gosforth, which has an even finer cross, this time built not by Anglo-Saxons, but by Vikings. This narrow cross soars skyward, representing Ysdragil, the sacred ash tree which held up the Viking world. It is surmounted by a wheelheaded cross, carved with Irish symbols of the Trinity. Thus pagan and Christian themes are combined.

Inside the nearby church are two hog-back tombs of similar date, carved with knotwork, figures, rings and serpents. Built into an arch is part of a 13th century grave and above parts of two old crosses, one showing men fishing. By the church is attractive Gosforth Hall. In the village itself the library building dates from 1628.

Next along the main road is Calder Bridge. Turn right along a minor road from here to see beautiful Calder Abbey, which in Springtime is set amidst a sea of flowers. It was founded in 1134 by monks from Furness, but their little church was destroyed by the Scots and, losing faith, the monks fled to found Byland Abbey in safer Yorkshire. Another party of Furness monks built the present abbey, which stands in the grounds of a private house.

A couple of miles along the road towards Ennerdale is Monks Bridge, built by the Calder monks.

Turn left at Calder Bridge and you're in a very different world. Calder Hall atomic power station, opened in 1956, was the world's first. The dome of an advanced gas-cooled reactor, built in 1963, is also prominent among the cooling towers and chimneys. Whatever your views on nuclear power, one thing is for certain. It makes a lot less mess than coal. Just go up the coast to Workington and see for yourself. Calder Hall and Windscale can be visited, if bookings are made in advance.

At Beckermet, to the west of the A595, the old church has two Saxon crosses in its grounds, both bear carvings. The smaller one has runes said to refer to "Edith, little maid".

Haile, on a minor road between Calder Bridge and Egremont, has a Georgian church with part of a Saxon cross. The tomb of John Ponsonby, who died in 1670, has an unusual rhyme beginning "Learn reader under this stone doth lye, A Rare example cald John Ponsonby". Haile Hall has datestones of 1591 and 1625.

Egremont has a broad, tree-lined street, and a castle on a mound. The castle was founded by William de Meschines, between 1130 and 1140 and gradually extended. It is open to the public.

St Bees, according to legend, gets its name from an Irish princess who faced shipwreck on the fierce cliffs of St Bees Head and vowed she would lead a life of prayer if saved. Granted safety she then asked the Lord of Egremont for land to build a nunnery and he, rather rashly knowing Lakeland weather, said she could have as much as was covered by snow on Midsummer Day. Three square miles at St Bees were covered. The Benedictines built a priory here and their fine Norman doorway can still be seen in the restored chancel.

Edmund Grindall, who became Archbishop of Canterbury in 1575, was born nearby and went to the priory school. When this was was closed through the Dissolution of the monasteries he founded a free grammar school to replace it. The fine Elizabethan building is now a public school.

8   Furness & Cartmel

Furness is the part of Cumbria that was originally Lancashire, separated by sea yet nontheless linked to the bigger part of the red rose county. This link was what used to be the main west coast highway, the sands route across Morecambe Bay. You can still take it now, for the Duchy of Lancaster maintains, as it has done for centuries, a Morecambe Bay guide. He is Mr Cedric Robinson, who on certain days takes parties across. It's an experience not to be missed: miles of trackless wilderness, untouched by man — that's providing they don't build the Morecambe Bay barrage.

The canons of Cartmel Priory grew rich from their control of this route. Cartmel village is one of Cumbria's historic showpieces. Picturesque cottages are grouped about the square, dominated by the ancient gatehouse of the priory. This fortified tower, built in the 14th century, has served the village as a court house and as a school. Now it is run as a small museum by the National Trust.

The priory, the village's chief glory, was founded by William Marshall for the Augustinian canons in 1188. The north door has dog tooth work of this date. The priory gradually grew until the end came with its dissolution in 1537. When the canons left the priory was unroofed and the weather began to take its toll. Its south choir was preserved, however, as the village church. In 1618 the whole church was reroofed, though the damage done by the rain can still be seen on some of the wonderful old choir stalls. At the same time the black oak screen of Flemish workmanship was installed.

Among points of special interest are the Harrington tomb of 1347, a rare Vinegar Bible, a first edition of Spenser's "Faerie Queen" and a 200-year-old umbrella to keep vicars dry at funerals.

Cark Hall, just before the B5277 coast road is reached, is a great rambling place which seems to have grown rather than been designed, and consequently has great charm. It is now several private homes, but from the road you can see its chief glory, a magnificently ornate doorway said to have been built by Robert Rawlinson as the replica of the one at his Oxford college.

Just up the B road is Holker Hall, a popular tourist attraction. It is a fine mansion, built mainly in Victorian times, but with a 17th century wing. Flookburgh is just a mile or so down the road and even the drab grey pebble dash can't hide its historic charm. It is every inch a Morecambe Bay fishing village and even the weather vane on the church is shaped to look like that peculiarly Morecambe Bay fish, the fluke. King Charles visited the town and dined on cockles at the Crown Inn. His great seal can be seen inside the church, along with ancient market regalia and two halberd heads, one of which is shaped – you've guessed it – like a fluke!

At the end of a lane is Cannon Winder, a rambling 16th century house marked by a particularly large chimney.

Just off the B5277 to the east of Flookburgh is Wraysholme Tower, a ruined limestone pele, attached to a farmhouse.

Grange-over-Sands is a genteel resort where great palace-like hotels line the wooded hillside. To its south is Guides Cottage, the traditional home of the Morecambe Bay guides.

On Hamps Fell, to the north, is the hospice, a viewpoint built by a Cartmel vicar in 1834.

At Lindale, on the A590, is a cast iron obelisk in memory of the ironmaster John Wilkinson, a remarkable man who sailed the world's first iron ship, though it was only a model, nearby. John's father, Isaac, was already in the iron business. The pair founded furnaces at Coalbrookdale in Shropshire, where they cast the parts of the famous Iron Bridge.

The Wilkinsons lived at Wilkinson House in the village and later at imposing Castlehead House, which is now St Mary's College. Fittingly John, who died in 1808, was buried in an iron coffin, though this was temporarily lost on the sands crossing.

At Witherslack, off the A590 to the east, St Paul's church seems to slumber in its idyllic setting beneath a limestone crag. It was built and endowed in 1649 by John Borwick, an ardent Royalist who later became Dean of St Paul's. It was one of the few churches to be built in these troubled times.

On the hillside to the north-west, reached by narrow lanes, is Cartmel Fell Church: one of the most magical little places in the whole of Cumbria, with a view across woodland and meadows to the Lakeland mountains beyond.

A proud boast of this parish is that it contains more damson trees than any other in the land. The tiny church, built in 1504, is dedicated to St Anthony. Inside is a three-decker pulpit of 1698, a beautifully carved screen and box pews, where the better off local families would sit. The glass in the east window was taken from Cartmel Priory and, on the left you see St Anthony. Fixed into the south wall is a tile-work picture of the saint, probably brought from Holland in the 17th century. In a corner is a sad little tombstone, with touching rhyme, to three-year-old Betty Poole. In the vestry is a unique wooden figure of Christ, part of the crucifix boasted by most churches before the Reformation.

At the porch entrance are grooves where churchgoers used to sharpen their arrows and, in the yard, is a mounting block with post where they would tether their horses during services.

At the bottom of the hill stands Hodge Hill, a beautiful old house with diamond-paned windows and a wooden spinning gallery where the fleece of the Herdwick sheep would be spun by the womenfolk to make thread for the famous Kendal green cloth.

Finsthwaite Church, reached by minor road from Newby Bridge and Lakeside, has a white cross on its south wall said to mark the final resting place of Princess Clementine Johannes Sobieski Douglas, an illegitimate child of Bonnie Prince Charlie. She lived at nearby Finsthwaite House and died in 1711. One of the staunchly Jacobite Towneley family erected the cross here last century. Also at Finsthwaite is the Stott Park Bobbin Mill, built in 1835 and a reminder of a traditional Lakeland industry. The densely wooded country of southern Lakeland, with its coppiced trees, is partly the result of this industry and others which used this source of wood.

Backbarrow, where the A590 runs through a wooded gorge, is well known for its "dolly blue" mill. But the mill was originally built for

Angry skies above Castlerigg stone circle, Keswick. (page 8)

The "inland sea" at Ravenglass. (page 11) ▼

▲ Walls Castle, the Roman bath house at Ravenglass. (page 11)

▼ The Ravenglass and Eskdale railway at Muncaster Mill. (page 11)

The water-wheel at Muncaster Mill. (pages 11 & 12)

Lonely Hall Waberthwaite Church. (page 12) Intricately carved Irton Cross. (page 13)

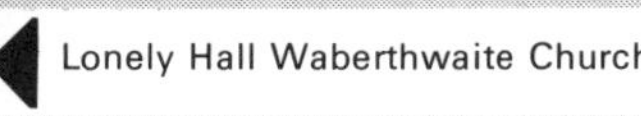

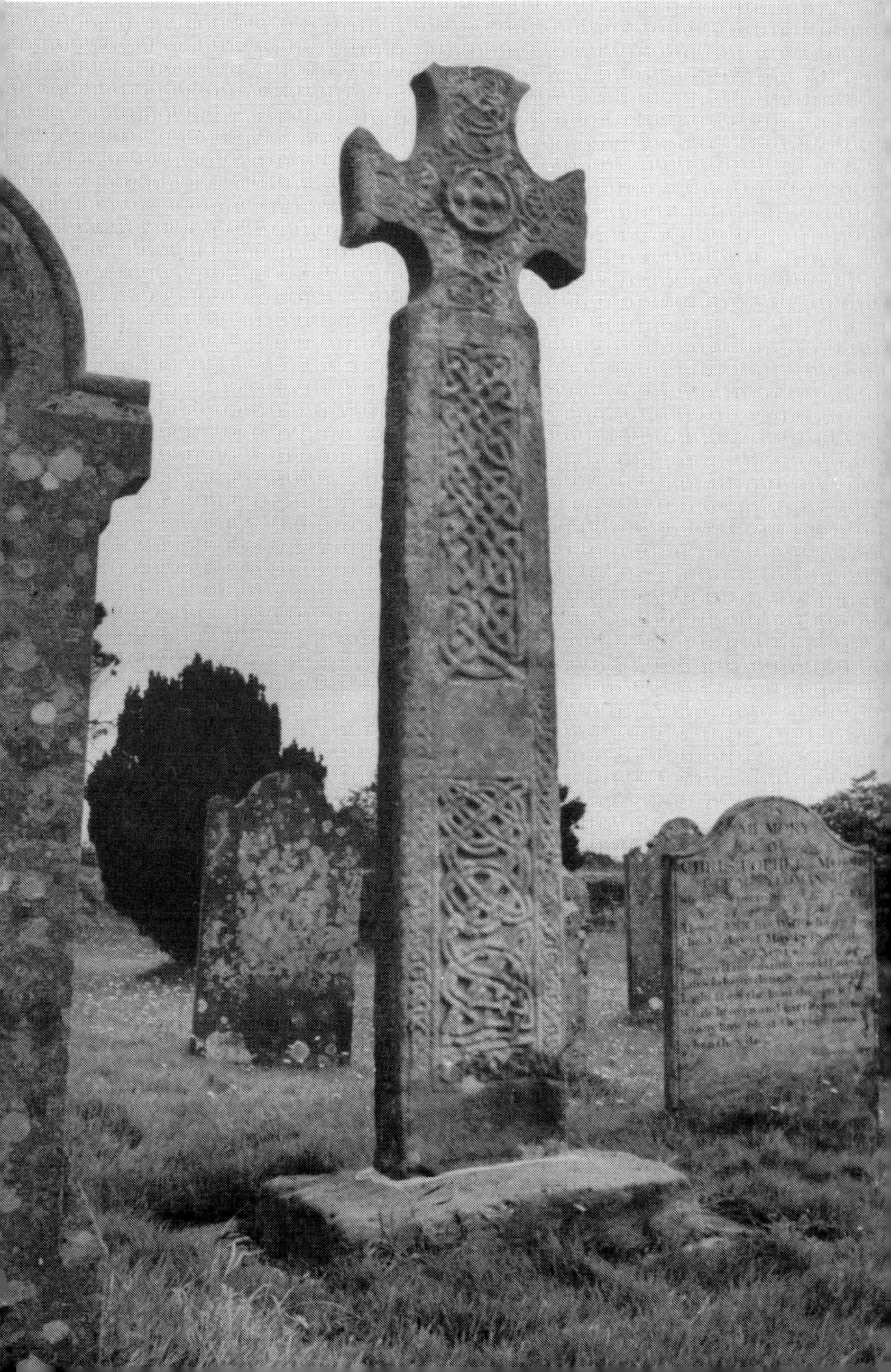

A mounted warrior in a detail from the cross.

Gosforth Cross combines Christian and pagan themes. (page 13) ▼

Calder Abbey in its peaceful wooded valley. (page 13)

weaving and won an evil reputation, because its owners used child labour from the London workhouses.

Ulverston has industry, but it has also got a group of 18th century buildings grouped attractively round its main square. On the Hill of Hoad to the north of the town, you can't miss what looks like a lighthouse that's lost its way. In fact the building, a replica of Smeaton's Eddystone Lighthouse, is a monument to Ulverston's greatest son: John Barrow.   Barrow was the son of a smallholder at Dragley Beck and was one of those men who seem to be always in the right place at the right time. Through hard work and helpful friends he became a leading geographer, a founding member of the Royal Geographic Society and second secretary to the Admiralty, where he encouraged voyages of exploration. He was made a baron and died in 1848. Charming Swarthmoor Hall, a mile to the south of Ulverston, was built in the early 17th century by a wealthy lawyer and judge, Thomas Fell. In 1652 George Fox, the roaming preacher who founded the Quaker movement, found refuge here after being driven from Ulverston church. Fell and his wife, Margaret, came under the preacher's spell and let him use the hall as a base.

For a time the influence of the Fells helped many persecuted Quakers, but even Margaret was eventually taken to the prison of Lancaster Castle, though later released. When Fell died she married Fox and they founded the nearby Friends Meeting House, which bears the legend "Ex Dono G.F. 1688" – the gift of George Fox. The Hall is open several days of the week.

At Pennington, on the other side of the A590, the church, though much rebuilt, bears witness to ancient times. A Norman Tympanum, set in the wall, bears runes saying "Gamel founded this church, Hubert the mason wrought". There is also a 1680 sundial.

At Urswick, to the south, St Mary's church was the original centre of Christianity in these parts. Inside is preserved part of an Anglo-Saxon cross and part of a Viking wheel-headed cross. A hagioscope, or peephole, built in the 13th century, allowed the congregation in the aisle to watch Communion. Also to be seen is a three-decker pulpit, a screen with carved figures and a window with stained glass from Furness Abbey. The east window bears the arms of Queen Mary, who held lands in these parts. Behind the altar is a painting of the Last Supper by local artist James Cranke.

Older even than Urswick are two stone circles, known as the "Druids Circle", on nearby Birkrigg Common.

On the A5087 coast road from Ulverston is Conishead Priory, built in the 12th century by Gamel de Pennington – we've already met him at Pennington church. Augustinian canons lived here guiding travellers across the Leven sands. On Chapel Island in the middle of the estuary is the remnant of the chapel they built. The present Conishead Priory is much less ancient, built for Thomas Bradyll in the gothic style about 200 years ago.

St Cuthbert's Church at Aldingham, further along the coast road, is said to cover the spot where the coffin of St Cuthbert lay when his remains were being carried away from Viking-devastated Northumbria. The church, dating back to the 12th and 13th centuries, has a very old font and a hagioscope.

Rampside Hall, another stage down the coast road, is noted for its impressive, diagonally-set chimneys, known as the "twelve apostles".

In the sea beyond neighbouring Roa Island is Piel Island, reached by boat from the village and built by the monks of Furness in 1327 to guard their sea trade. In 1487 the Pretender Lambert Simnel landed here, masquerading as Edward Earl of Warwick and challenging Henry VII for the throne. He was defeated and spent the rest of his life in the royal kitchens.

In a room at the island's Ship Inn is a chair. The penalty of sitting here is a round of drinks, but you may become a knight of Piel, with the privilege of being looked after should you be shipwrecked here.

At Barrow there's a touch of Glasgow, where the red sandstone flats of Old Barrow, built for shipyard workers in the 1880's, look just like Glasgow tenements. At the time they were thought to be model dwellings for the working classes.

Leaving Barrow by the A590, on the right is Furness Abbey, a great red sandstone pile lying in the romantically wooded Vale of the Deadly Nightshade-Bekansgill. It was founded in 1127 by King Stephen and its Cistercian monks grew rich on the Lakeland wool trade. A line of Norman arches is particularly impressive and there is a well-preserved chapter house, an infirmary – with effigies of knights – and sewage system, as well as the noble ruins of the great church.

The Railway Hotel nearby is built on the foundations of the manor put up by Thomas Preston, who bought the valley when the abbey was suppressed. There are also two ancient pack-horse bridges over the little river.

At Dalton-in-Furness the old pele tower in the centre was the manorial court of the abbots of Furness, later it became the town's court house. Now the National Trust owns it and it is open to the public.

Broughton-in-Furness has an attractive market square with an 18th century town hall and an obelisk erected in 1810. The church contains some Norman work but the finest building locally is Broughton Tower: an elegant home built, like so many others, around a pele tower.

About two miles beyond the River Duddon a minor road leaves the A595 to the right. After almost a mile a rough track leads up the hillside to remote Swinside stone circle. This great prehistoric achievement must be the least visited of England's large stone circles. It is more than 90 ft across and consists of more than 50 great grey stones. It is sometimes known as "Sunkenkirk".

Millom Castle and church lie just to the north of industrial Millom. The attractive church dates back to Norman times and its unusual west window in the shape of an oval is known as the "fish window". Towering above the church is the castle, a pele tower on the grand scale.

At Kirksanton on the A5093 to the west stand two standing stones; one with a marking, known as the Giant's Grave.

Hodbarrow is on the coast south of Millom. Here deposits of iron ore were discovered and worked until as recently as 1968. Still to be seen are the mighty sea walls which enabled ore to be won from the very edge of the sea.

9   *Around* Kendal

Kendal is a place you can only really explore on foot, for half the charm of this white, limestone town is the little alleyways, or wynds, which lead off the main streets: Stricklandgate and Highgate. There are many more of them, despite ill-advised clearance, than a book this size can mention, just find them for yourself. You won't be disappointed. My own favourite is opposite the town hall, under an archway dated 1659 which leads onto a pleasant courtyard with almshouses. In the wall is a black iron offertory box with an injunction to "Remember the Poore".

Kendal's Holy Trinity Church, on the river bank, is a building expressive of the columns and monuments to local families. In the altar are tombs to three of the greatest families: the Stricklands, Bellinghams and Parrs. One of the Parrs was Katherine, last and luckiest wife of Henry VIII – for she outlived him. In the sanctuary is a brass plate to Raulph Tirer, a former vicar, who died in 1627. It's worth reading and begins "London bredd me, Westminster fedd me . . . .".

Nearby Abbot Hall, Kendal's well-known art and exhibition centre, gets its name because it stands on the site of a former abbey. It was built in 1759 by Col. George Wilson, of Dallam Tower, Milnthorpe, as a town house for him and his family.

Other Kendal buildings of note are old hotels which grew up on the pack horse and coaching trades. The White Hart is probably the oldest, but the 17th century Fleece is equally fine.

Kendal has been associated with many industries, among them the manufacture of snuff and mint cake. Projecting from a wall in Stricklandgate a hog with a bristled back advertises another: brush-making.

In Wildman Street, near the rail station, are two old snuff factories. Also there is the Castle Dairy, which incorporates a peculiar old building about 600 years old.

To the east of the town the imposing ruins of Kendal Castle can be seen on its enormous mound. This was the home of the Parrs, including Katharine, who married Henry in 1543.

To the south of the town, on Collin Road, Collinfield House stands amid semi-detached suburbia. Built in 1663 it was the home of the Sedgwicks, one of whom was private secretary to Lady Anne Clifford, Countess of Pembroke, who gave him a lock bearing her initials which can still be seen on the studded oak door.

On Castle Howe, which rises above the hospital on the west of the town, is an 18th century monument to Liberty. The howe itself is the remains of an old motte and bailey castle.

The minor road beyond the hospital leads to Brigsteer, over the Helsington Barrows, a limestone hill where the soil is so scarce that vegetation struggles to find a foothold. On the summit, to the left of the road, is simple St John's Church, which offers lovely views to those who stop here.

South of Kendal on the A6 is Sizergh Castle and gardens, looked after by the National Trust and open to the public. Sizergh is an ancient pele tower with Elizabethan additions and has been the home of the Stricklands since 1239. It's one of Cumbria's finest homes and among the more memorable features are Elizabethan woodwork and a portable altar of painted Italian leather. The gardens provide the perfect foil for the house and its outbuildings. Sizergh was the home of Katharine Parr after Henry's death.

About two miles further down the A6 is another ancient home

built, like Sizergh, around a pele tower kernel. This is Levens Hall, which is also open to the public. The gardens here are even more notable, with their famous topiary. The gardens were created by Mons Beaumont who came from the "Sun King's" palace at Versailles, but one tree, known as the "Great Umbrella", is much older; said to date back 800 years. Also on show in the grounds is a collection of steam engines.

Levens began life when Matthew de Redman built a pele tower here in the 14th century. In 1562 the Bellingham family bought it, but it passed from their grasp when Alan Bellingham had to find money to pay his vast gambling debts. Now it is the home of the Bagots, and a very elegant home too, with fine paintings, a collection of harpsichords, Gillow furniture and many items of silver.

A mile south is Heversham, a village by-passed by the main road, where St Peter's Church contains a fine fragment of an Anglo-Saxon preaching cross, decorated with birds and animals. On the opposite side of the A6, attractive Heversham Hall dates back to the 14th century.

Even more attractive is Hincaster Hall, reached by minor roads to the east of Heversham. It has great mullioned windows and those ponderous chimney stacks so familiar in Lakeland homes. Near Stainton, on the other side of the rail line, another fine old house is Sellet Hall.

Around here can be seen the sad reminder of the once proud Lancaster Canal. The last few miles of this canal, built in 1819, are drained and a lower section which still has water has no boats, because it is sealed off from the main canal to the south by the M6. At Hincaster is a canal tunnel and at Sedgwick to the north a fine aqueduct.

Attractive Milnthorp village on the A6 has an 18th century market cross. To the south-east set in grounds you can drive through is Dallam Tower, built in 1720 for the Wilson family. A highlight is the herd of fallow deer which even have an elegant stone-pillared building to shelter them.

At Beetham on the A6 south of Milnthorpe, there's plenty to see just a few yards from the main road. St Michael's Church in its trim churchyard was founded in Norman times, but is built mainly in later gothic styles. There is some old stained glass and some interesting monuments. In Parsonage Farm near the church, there is a blocked-up medieval doorway. The village also has some elegant Georgian houses and two grander homes: Ashton House and Beetham House.

Reached by a footbridge across the River Bela is Heron Mill, an old water mill that has been put back into working order by a trust and which can be visited during the summer months. Evidently the monks of Conishead Priory were the first people to mill here, as long ago as 1220. There's been a mill here ever since, the present one being built about 1750. It has four millstones driven by its wheel.

Just south of Beetham 17th century Beetham Hall stands midst the ruins of an older, fortified manor house.

South of the little coastal town of Arnside the impressive shell of Arnside Tower, a 15th century pele which sheltered locals from marauding Scots and pirates, has a commanding position. The walls are more than 50 ft high.

To the west of Arnside there are remains of another pele tower at Hazelslack.

Burton-in-Kendal is spoiled by the busy A6070, which runs through its heart, but even the noise and fumes fail to hide its history. The church was founded in Norman times and the remains of Anglo-Saxon crosses show worship on this site went back even further. The church also has an ornately carved Jacobean pulpit. A notable building in the main street is supported by columns and in the square is the 18th century market cross.

North of Kendal beautiful Long Sleddale, reached by minor road from the A6 at Watchgate, shelters historic Ubarrow Hall: an ancient pele attached to a cottage. Obviously even the remoteness of a place like this was insufficient protection from the Scots.

Burneside to the east of the A591 Windermere road, is a workaday place with plenty of character. The road to the village is marked by a monument built in 1814 to honour William Pitt "the pilot that weathered the storm". Further along is Tolson House, built by a wealthy leather merchant in 1638. Another old House, the Hollins built in 1687, is also on this side of the village. Burneside has a very fine pele tower at Burneside Hall to the east, the number of such buildings indicating the insecurity of life in this region. Attached to the pele is a 14th century house where, no doubt, owner and tenants lived when times were peaceful, to retreat into the tower at the sign of danger. Near here is Oakbank Mill, built in the 1840's for bobbin making.

10 ᶜKirkby Lonsdale

Overlooked by the fells of Yorkshire, Kirkby Lonsdale still has a very Cumbrian flavour and has a claim to being the most attractive town in the region. Here you can see Devil's Bridge, which has been described as one of the finest ancient bridges in the country, its three graceful arches spanning the Lune at a romantic place where swirling waters meet glistening rocks. Legend says the bridge was built by the Devil, but at the south-east corner a stone bears the inscription "Fear God and Honour the King 1633" and also "W . . . N Constable of Lonsdal".

The bridge is a somewhat overcrowded tourist attraction, but at least this keeps the town centre from getting busier than it already is. The church of St Mary is reached through massive gates and stands in one of the most picturesque yards imagineable. The church itself is Norman and was owned by St Mary's Abbey at York. In the tower is an impressive Norman doorway, with the dog tooth work so beloved at that time. Inside are six Norman columns.

In the churchyard, swathed in stands of daffodils in spring, is a viewing tower known as Ruskin's View; for the prospect from here was rightly praised by Ruskin and painted by Turner. Also to be seen close by is the mound or motte, where a castle once stood guarding the crossing of the Lune.

From Ruskin's View it is an enjoyable stroll down to the river bank and then, through meadows and past the town's miniature gas-holder to emerge on Mill Brow, a picturesque street leading up to the Market Square. On one side of the lane is the old market cross with a stone ball on its apex. Back in the main street the Sun Inn leans out into the street like someone who has drunk too freely of the local beer. It is supported on three huge, rounded pillars. From Ruskin's View you can see Underley Hall to the north. Built in 1825 it is now a school.

North along the A683 Sedberg road is Middleton Hall, a 15th century building in the shape of an "H" and a lovely example of old Cumbria. On the other bank of the Lune, Rigmaden Hall is falling into ruin.

Not far away is another of those links with the beginning of the Quaker sect in which Cumbria is so rich. A minor road north from the junction of the B6256 and the A684 Kendal–Sedbergh road takes you to the lonely graveyard where once stood Firbank Church. The atmosphere somehow tells you that great events took place here in spite of its present tranquility. A tablet on the nearby rock is more explicit, explaining that George Fox stood here to preach to hundreds of local people, to give what must be one of the most famous sermons in British history. Now the rock is known as Fox's Pulpit. (For more about Fox read the section on Furness.)

11 Penrith & the Vale of Eden

The rich Vale of Eden with its lush green meadows, its gentle and prosperous lowland villages, is in stark contrast to much of barren Cumbria. At its heart is Penrith, the ancient capital of the region.

The town is overlooked by the Beacon, the present structure which was built in 1719 replacing an earlier one. Warnings blazed from here when invasion threatened. The last time was in 1745 when Bonnie Prince Charlie came south.

On the other side of the town the castle, built when war was an ever-present threat, slumbers peacefully now in the town's park. It was once the home of Warwick the Kingmaker and later Richard of Gloucester; ill-omened Richard III lived here extending the castle during his tenure. Penrith citizens, in the days before they had regard for their heritage, used the castle as a convenient quarry for building stone but an impressive portion remains and can be visited freely.

In the town the Gloucester Arms in Great Dockray was built in 1477. Richard may also have lived here for his sign – two rampant boars – is on the front of the building. Another old pub is the Two Lions Inn built in 1585 as a town house for Gerald Lowther.

St Andrew's Church is a fine Georgian building with a much older tower. In its yard the Giants Grave is two tall crosses with four hogback graves. Another stone that has stood here for 1,000 years is known as the "Giant's Thumb". There are some interesting buildings around the churchyard, one of which has connections with Wordsworth (see later section). Other interesting buildings are to be found on Sandgate. Bowerbank Hall has an inscription over the doorway to say it was built by John Matthews in 1612. Sandgate Hall, built 30 years later, was the town house of the Fletchers of Hutton-in-the-Forest.

Penrith Town Hall in Corney Street was designed by Robert Adam. Not far away the George Hotel provided lodgings for Bonnie Prince Charlie on his march south. One of the few men whose names have become part of the English language, grew up at Page Hall in Foster Street. He was Samuel Plimsoll, who must have saved thousands of seamen's lives with his line that warns ships of overloading, but who achieved more fame through his innovation in footwear.

In a field to the south of the town is the Plague Stone, a square block with a hollow in it. In 1598 when the plague claimed the lives of 2,000 local people, business continued, with traders taking the precaution of placing money in disinfectant in the stone's hollow.

Just south of Penrith on the A66, is Brougham Castle towering over the River Eamont. It was built on the site of a Roman fort in 1170 and later extended by the indefatigable Lady Anne Clifford, who merits a special section to this book. It is open to the public. Nearby is St Ninian's Church, known as "Ninekirks". Lady Anne restored this fine country church in 1660 and her initials can be seen over the altar.

Also at Brougham and also restored by Lady Anne is tiny St Wilfrid's Church, which has a sumptious interior of carved woodwork and screens, with a triptych attributed to Durer. Another treasure is a magnificently carved locker.

Arthur's Round Table is a prehistoric earthwork, 150 ft in diameter, surrounded by a ditch. Nearby Mayburgh is another prehistoric earthwork, oval in shape, with a large standing stone in the middle.

Dalemain, home of the Hasells, stands on the B5320 Ullswater Road, built of stone the pale pink of a maiden's blush. Open to the public it is an old house given a graceful exterior in Georgian times.

Dacre, reached by minor road from the B5320 or B5288, is one of those endearing places where history seems to live on rather than be preserved. Dacre castle is a 14th century pele tower, attractively set in a small garden. It is a family home which can be visited by appointment. St Andrew's Church dates back to Norman times and has a lock on the door given by Lady Anne and bearing her initials and the date 1661. Also to be seen are two Anglo-Saxon cross fragments with carvings. One may show King Athelstan and King Constantine meeting at Dacre to sign an agreement in 926.

Hutton John, south-east of Penruddock, is an old pele tower gradually converted over the centuries into a rather unusual looking home. It has gardens laid out in Tudor times with sombre-looking yews and can be visited by appointment.

Greystoke, on the A594, is an interesting old place with a vast old church. St Andrew's dates back to 1382 and has a fine set of miserichords and other items of interest. In the lane to the church is a stone protected by a grille. Known as the "Sanctuary Stone" this marked the line beyond which fugitives could feel safe under the protection of the church.

Greystoke Castle is a pele tower which grew into a stately home, being finally rebuilt and restored last century. The 11th Duke of Norfolk, who lived here, built three farms which look like no others in the land. They lie to the east of Greystoke, by the A594. Fort Putnam and Bunker's Hill get their names from the American War of Independence, while Spire House bears the reason for its name on the roof. Johnby Hall, on the minor road north of Greystoke, is another old pele tower converted into a home in 1583.

Hutton-in-the-Forest, lying between the B5305 and the A6, is another ancient home which began life as a pele. A medieval hall was added and then the Fletcher family, which bought the estate in 1606, built much in the Jacobean style. It is now the home of Lord Inglewood and can be visited by appointment.

At Armathwaite, on the other side of the A6 and on the banks of the River Eden, stands the Chapel of Christ and St Mary which fell into disrepair and was restored 300 years ago by Richard Skelton of Armathwaite Castle. The castle occupies a romantic spot over-looking the river.

At Staffield, south by minor road, the Nunnery Walks leads into an overgrown gorge, where some ancient stonework from the original nunnery can still be seen.

At Kirkoswald on the B6413 the tower of St Oswald's Church is some 200 yards from the rest of the building. The church is dedicated to St Oswald but almost certainly this was a sacred spot before Christianity reached these islands. For, bubbling out from underneath the nave, is a spring, at one time no doubt a holy well. St Oswald's used to be a collegiate church but the college became the home of the Featherstonhaugh family.

There's another interesting church at Great Salkeld on the B6412, which has a fortified tower to provide protection from marauding Scots. The tower is entered through a cunningly-devised gate of ironwork, made in the 14th century.

Little Meg lies by the minor road from Kirkoswald to Langwathby. It is a circle of 11 stones, two decorated with cup and ring markings. Nearby, reached by a tiny lane, is big sister: Long Meg and her Daughters, which is probably the finest to be seen anywhere without going to Salisbury Plain. The Daughters, fifty-one stones, some of them of great size and weighing many tons, form a circle more than 350 ft in diameter. Outside the ring Long Meg is a great finger of stone pointing to the sky. A cup and ring marking can be seen near its base. For some reason various different sorts of stones are used, and several must have been brought from some distance.

Just down the road, the water mill at Little Salkeld is open to visitors, who can watch the two cast iron waterwheels turning slowly in the mill race and see the ponderous machinery turn grain into flour. It is a fascinating place to visit.

Edenhall, south-west of Langwathby, has a Norman church on Saxon foundations and contains monuments to the Musgrave family.

The church at Long Marton, to the east of the A66, has stones with ancient symbols carved on them. One of the chancel walls slopes outwards, representing Christ's head hanging down at the crucifixion, it is said.

At Bolton, on the other side of the A road, All Saints Church is a small Norman building. One Norman doorway is blocked-up, with a window in it. In the wall above can be seen a carving of knights jousting. There is also a finely-wrought chancel screen.

Appleby is an ancient borough and one of Cumbria's loveliest little towns. It was home to Lady Anne Clifford and formerly the county town of Westmorland, and wears its history and importance with pride, even if progress has rather passed it by.

At one end of the main street is the castle, at the other end the equally fine parish church, which is dedicated to St Lawrence. It is built in the Early English style and has interesting monuments and a 15th century screen. (More about both castle and church appear in the section on Lady Anne.)

A prominent feature of Boroughgate, as the main street is called, is the Low Cross, which was built in the 18th century. A similar pillar, outside the castle, bears the inscription "Retain your loyalty, Preserve your rights". In the Market Place can be seen a bull ring, where an unfortunate creature would be tethered while it was "baited" by dogs, for the amusement of the populace. Also to be seen is the Moot Hall, built in 1596, where the burghers used to meet and, on the left hand side of the street, the "White House", built by Jack Robinson – the man whose name has become a byword for swiftness. Robinson was Mayor of Appleby before embarking on a career in national politics which made him Secretary to the Treasury.

The church at Great Ormeside, 2½ miles south of Appleby, is set in a commanding position on a knoll overlooking the Eden. It is a Norman church, with fortified tower to protect parishioners in times of invasion.

Brough, where the A66 and A685 meet, has perhaps the most striking castle in Cumbria. There are considerable remains of the keep, built in 1170, fortifications from later periods and paved courtyards. The castle is set on a hill to the south of the town. It suffered damage by the Scots in 1521, but was repaired, like so much else, by the ubiquitous Lady Anne. Cared for nowadays by the Department of the Environment, it is well worth a visit.

Kirkby Stephen, on the A685, gets its name from the parish church of St Stephen, an impressive old building with fortified tower, which contains some interesting monuments.

To the south of the town is partly-ruined Wharton Hall, fallen from its days of grace and now a farmhouse. Built in the 15th century round a courtyard, it was once – as its name suggests – the home of the Whartons.

By the side of the road through quiet Mallerstangdale, stands Pendragon Castle: a Norman pele tower whose name links it to Arthurian legend, for Uther Pendragon was said to be Arthur's father. On the other side of the infant Eden, Lammerside Castle is another ruinous pele tower. At Ravenstonedale, just off the A685, St Oswald's church is worth a visit. It was rebuilt in 1744 in Puritan style, so that the congregation were facing each other during services. There is also a three-decker pulpit.

Tebay is a railway town, a bleak and rather forbidding place, which nevertheless still retains something of the taste of those bold days when men were forging an iron network across the country and reducing travelling time from days to hours.

To the north, on the B6260, is rural Orton, where All Saints Church, a 13th century building, and Orton Old Hall, in the main street, are both worth a peep.

Shap, on the A6, tends to be remembered as the last staging post before the grim journey over Shap Fell, or rather what could be a grim journey in the days when motor vehicles were less reliable and before the M6 motorway was built. But Shap has some surprises to offer those willing to turn aside from the main road. To the west there's the proud remains of Shap Abbey, now looked after by the Department of the Environment. It was founded by Premonstratensian canons around 1199, though most of the buildings which remain are of a slightly later date, and the most eye-catching feature is the early 16th century tower.

Nearby, the Thunder Stone once marked the end of an avenue of stones leading to a stone circle south of Shap village. The remains of this circle can be seen between the A6 and the rail line. There is another stone circle to the north of the village.

Keld Chapel, at the end of the minor road south west from the village, is a beautifully simple place of worship now cared for by the National Trust.

Askham, west of the A6 to the north of Shap, is a spacious and attractive village. Askham Hall is the 14th century home of the Sandford family, built around a courtyard and incorporating a great, fortified tower for refuge in times of trouble.

Nearby stands Lowther Castle, or rather the sad remains of a dream castle. The original castle was burnt in 1720, and Robert Adam was asked to design a grand castellated mansion. Adam's castle was never built, for it was decided to build an even grander castle to the design of an architect named Smirke. Unfortunately this great building was never to be finished and so it stands, one of the most spectacular shells to be seen anywhere.

By the castle is St Michael's Church and nearby is Lowther New Town, a late 17th century planned village built by Sir John Lowther. Another model settlement is Lowther Village, built, about a century later, by Robert Adam when he was designing the castle.

On the A6 at Hackthorpe is Jacobean Hackthorpe Hall.

---

12   Carlisle, Solway & the Border

Carlisle has been a border town for the best part of 2,000 years and, although things may be peaceful at the moment, it still wears a brooding air of watchfulness. In the past the citizens of Carlisle have had good reason to be watchful, whether they lived in what was Roman Luguvallum, British Caerleol, or in later medieval times. Always they have been watching to the north, across the rivers and the flat moss lands to Scotland.

Carlisle guards the crossing place over the River Eden: the gateway from Scotland into England. The Romans built a fortress here, but it's the Norman castle and cathedral that catch the eye nowadays.

The castle stands on a headland above the river crossing and is a museum of the Border Regiment. The first castle, probably built of wood, was built by William II. Later Carlisle passed into Scottish hands and King David I of Scotland built more formidable fortifications; to the later regret of his countrymen, for it was to prove a thorn in their sides for years once the English had regained the city.

The English were back in charge by 1157 and Henry II had the keep and curtain wall built. This basic structure of the castle has been added to and repaired from time to time over the centuries. The castle is open to visitors and is well worth a visit. Not to be missed are the wonderful carvings made by prisoners here 500 years ago. In 1569 Mary Queen of Scots was prisoner here. Another famous prisoner was Kinmont Willie, held here after being treacherously captured during a truce. His rescue by the Bold Buccleugh is celebrated in Scots ballad. A more peace-loving inmate of the castle dungeons was George Fox, the Quaker, who was "almost eaten to death by lice", but still found the prisoners "very loving and subject to me and some of them were convinced of the Truth".

Carlisle was for King Charles in the Civil War, but fell to the Scottish troops of General David Leslie after a long seige which saw the garrison feeding their horses with thatch and then finally eating their beasts. The Royalists regained Carlisle for a time, but, in 1648, they could not prevent Cromwell making a triumphant entry. The castle's last taste of war came in 1745 when it was taken by Bonnie

Prince Charlie and later held out forlornly for a time, under the command of Col Towneley, as the Prince retreated northwards to Culloden and defeat.

Carlisle's proudest possession is its cathedral, the second smallest in the country, but rivalling some of its bigger brothers in interest. The city was made a bishopric in 1133. Parts of the original Norman cathedral survive, recognised from the grey stones, possibly purloined from the Roman wall, with which it was built. Later work is in dark red sandstone. In the 13th century the cathedral was twice stricken by fire and there was much rebuilding. Later, during the seige of Carlisle, much more of the oiriginal building suffered when it was used to strengthen the town's defences. Only two of the original seven Norman bays survive. Inside the cathedral it is the windows, especially the nine lights of the east window, and the carved screens that catch the eye. Look out also for scenes depicting the seasons of the year carved in the capitals of the columns. A stone head above the pulpit is said to be king's favourite Piers Gaveston.

The choir stalls have ornately carved canopies, but look underneath the seats where the misericords, showing grinning monsters and other strange creatures, are particularly good. On the stallbacks are paintings showing the lives of the apostles and various saints.

Sir Walter Scott married Charlotte Carpenter in the cathedral in 1797. A house in nearby Castle Street bears a plaque to record that Scott slept here on the night before the wedding.

The buildings around the cathedral are known as "The Abbey", recalling the fact that Augustinian canons built their priory here at the beginning if the 11th century. The Fratry, built about 1482, was where the canons used to eat. It now houses the cathedral library. Another reminder of the priory is the gatehouse, bearing a Latin inscription to record its foundation by Prior Slee. Beyond this are the buildings of the cathedral precinct. There's the registry, the Georgian canonry and the Dean House, which is built round an older pele tower.

Carlisle's greatest days were the days of border warfare. The union of England and Scotland meant better times for the rest of the country, but leaner years for Carlisle, which sank from its former importance.In Georgian times it was a typical prosperous, but relatively small, country town. In Victorian times an attempt was made to restore Carlisle's fortunes through the Industrial Revolution, but these were never more than partly successful.

Although the town has its share of modern redevelopment, plenty survives from each of these eras. In Abbey Street are several fine

Georgian buildings. The pride of Castle Street is the Jacobean house built for Thomas Tullie. In 1689 Tullie became Dean of Carlisle. His home is now the city museum and library. It has a good collection of Roman antiquities.

Well worth a look is the 15th century tithe barn, built by Prior Gondibour, in the corner of St Cuthbert's churchyard. This stored the dues, paid in agricultural produce, to the church. Nearby is a section of Carlisle's medieval city wall, known as the West Wall.

Not to be missed in a tour of the city is the timber-framed Guild Hall, with its overhanging upper storey. Another fine building is the old Town Hall, built in 1717. At the bottom of its steps is Carlisle's Market Cross, erected in 1682. It bears a sundial and on the top, a lion holding a book. Important announcements were made here and in 1745 Bonnie Prince Charlie had his father proclaimed King James III of England.

At Junction Street the imposing Shaddon works were an attempt to introduce that golden goose, the cotton industry, to Carlisle. But it laid fewer golden eggs here than in Lancashire and the city became better known for its biscuits than its textiles.

Another industrial remain is the terminus of the Carlisle Canal, just west of Caldewgate. Old warehouses can be seen where barges docked to unload their wares.

Cumbria by the Solway is a world of its own: a world of broad horizons, spreading grasslands and expanses of mud and sand. Here the old Viking method of haaf net fishing for salmon is still carried out and sheep graze the famous Cumberland turf on which so many of Britain's great sporting events have been played. To get here take the B5307 from Carlisle and then branch off right along the road to Burgh-by-Sands.

At Burgh that great warrior King Edward I died on his way to meet the threat of Robert the Bruce. If he had been able to go on it is unlikely the "Hammer of the Scots", as Edward was known, would have failed in the way that Edward II did. There would have been no Bannockburn and Scottish history would have lost its most glorious chapter. A 20 ft pillar, surmounted by a cross, marks the spot where Edward died just over a mile to the north of the village.

In the village itself St Michael's Church has a somewhat warlike look, with its squat tower built so that villagers could shelter here in times of Scottish invasion. The church, like so many border buildings, is built from that convenient quarry the Roman wall. Parts of the church date back to Norman times, but look in particular for the "yatt", the iron gate, which defends access to the tower.

Next stop along the road is Drumburgh where the so-called castle

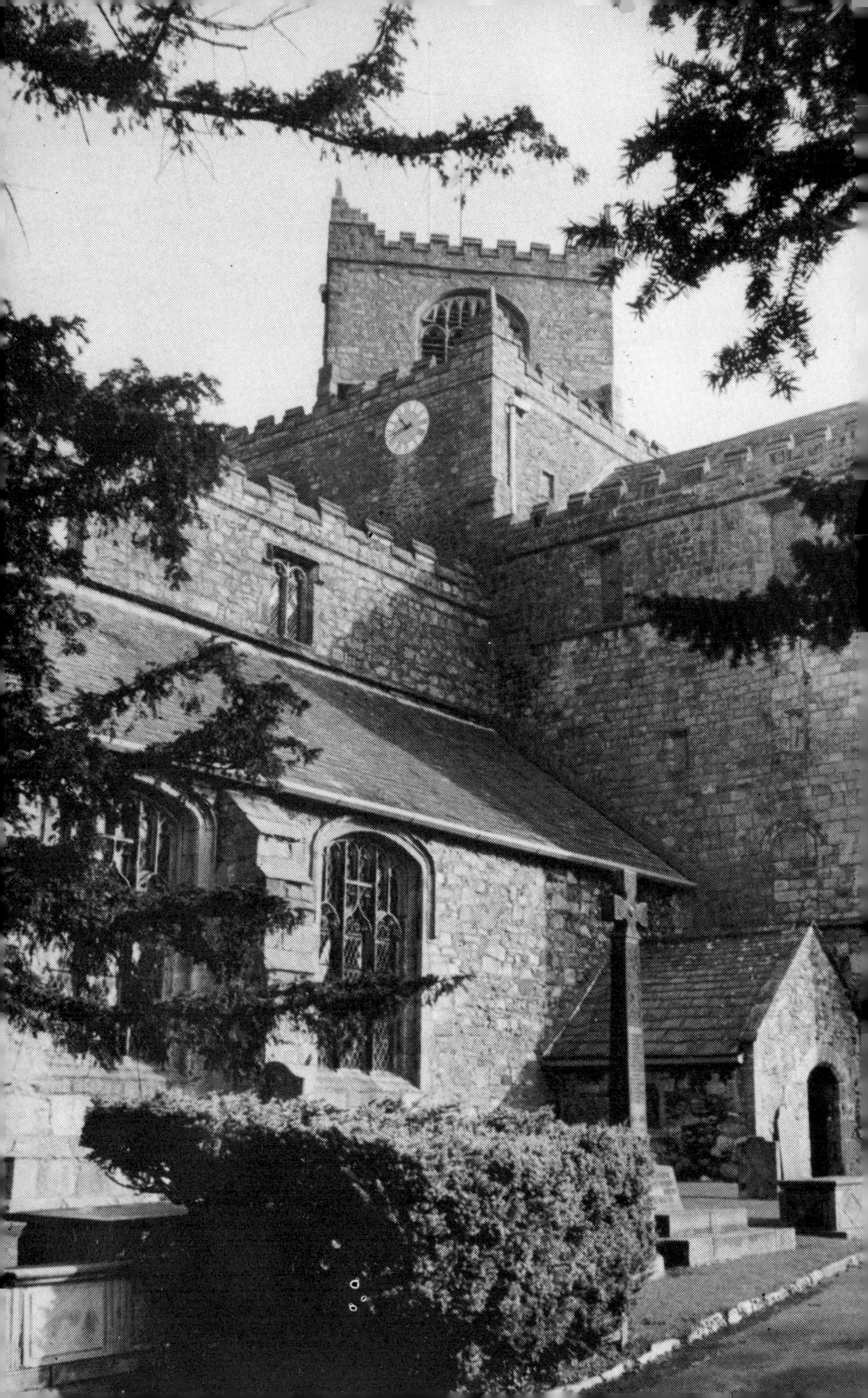

Cartmel Priory. (page 14)

The imposing doorway of Cark Hall. (page 15)

Cartmel Fell Church. (page 16)

Furness Abbey (page 18)

Kendal almshouses. (page 19)

Sizergh Castle. (page 20)

Moated Penrith Castle. (page 24)

Hodge Hill with its spinning gallery. (page 16)

Swarthmoor Hall. (page 17)

Inside Cartmel Fell Church.

Penrith churchyard. (page 25)

Dalemain House. (page 25)

Dacre Castle. (page 25)

Barre Castle
PRIVATE

Long Meg and Her Daughters. (page 27)

Appleby main street. (page 27)

Little Salkeld Mill. (page 27)

ne of the two water-wheels at Little Salkeld Mill. ▼ St Lawrence's Church, Appleby. (page 27)

"Remember the Poor Widows" and "Remember the Poore", says this offertory box in a Kendal passageway. (page 19) ▼

is a manor house built in 1307 and fortified in the reign of Henry VII by Lord Dacre. It guarded a ford across the Solway.

Going towards Bowness one comes to Fishers Cross, grandiosely known as Port Carlisle, where the Carlisle canal entered the sea. The canal, 11¼ miles long, linked Carlisle to the sea. It was built between 1819 and 1823 at a cost of £90,000, but never paid its way and was replaced by a railway in 1854. The stone bed of the canal now wears a sad air.

At Bowness are remains of another failed dream: a railway link to Scotland spanning the Solway sands. When this great viaduct was built, trains could avoid the detour around the head of the estuary. The viaduct was badly damaged by storms and gradually fell into disrepair, though thirsty Scots still used it on Sundays to enjoy a good English pint when their own pubs were closed. The viaduct was finally demolished in the 1930's, but the embankment still remains.

Bowness marked the end of the Roman Wall and the village is built on the site of a Roman fort. An altar to Jupiter can be seen in the wall of a roadside barn and a tablet of the 2nd Augustan Legion is to be seen in the wall of another building. St Michael's Church is Norman and has a fine font of this period. It is said the church bells were plundered from Scotland after the original bells had been taken by raiding Scots and then lost as the Solway tides overwhelmed them on the crossing of the sands.

There's another Norman church, St Bride's, at Kirkbride, the next village along the coast, where there's a moving inscription by a former vicar who lost his wife and six children in a cholera outbreak in 1746, yet still kept his faith in his Lord.

Newton Arlosh, the next stop, has a fortified church built by monks from nearby Holme Cultram Abbey. This Abbey was founded by Cistercian monks from Scotland in 1150, but only about a third of it survives, as the parish church of Abbeytown. The father of Robert the Bruce is buried here, under a stone marked with a cross, but that didn't stop his son pillaging here on one of his border forays.

Another building worth looking at is mullioned-windowed Mill-grove House, built in 1664, to the south of the church. A mile to the north of the village is Raby Cote Farm, where the monks of Holm Cultram farmed. Look at the farm wall and you will see stone carvings from the abbey, including an inscription built in upside down!

Going inland to Bromfield, St Mungo's Church has much Norman work and cross fragments even older. There are many interesting tombs and, in the adjacent field, is the Holy Well of St

Mungo in a small building. Quite probably the well was sacred in Celtic times and the church merely made it a more respectable place of pilgrimage by claiming it as its own.

Wigton, on the A596, is the capital of this little land, but its most interesting features date only from last century. Don't miss Highmoor House, to which a tower more than 130 ft tall was added in 1887 by its owner; a man who made his fortune selling clothing to Australia. In the Market Place the memorial fountain bears four reliefs which would do justice to Renaissance Italy.

On the ridge near Old Carlisle farmhouse, 1½ miles southeast, lies the Roman fort of Old Carlisle. A few traces still remain.

At Caldbeck, on the B5299, you're under the shadow of the fells. The main attraction here lies in the churchyard where can be seen the recently-vandalised grave of that most famous of huntsmen John Peel. I'm not a hunting supporter myself, but I wouldn't object to a pack of hounds being set on the trail of the people who did this.

The song that made Peel famous was written by his friend John Woodcock Graves. On the subject of verse, visit Low Brownrigg, a mile to the north of the village, where the mullion-windowed house has a moving little inscription over the doorway.

At Sebergham, on the B5305, the castle looks rather light-hearted in comparison to most of the grim northern strongholds. The reason is that this is a folly, built in the 18th century. St Mary's Church has some notable monuments with Latin inscriptions and fine sculpture.

Rose Castle, just off the B5299, is the historic home of the bishops of Carlisle. A castle is a fitting home for this fighting breed whose own brand of the "church militant" used to include a bit of border raiding. Although the castle dates from the 13th century it has been extensively altered over the years.

Thistlewood Tower, about 2 miles to the south, is less impressive, but more authentic, being a pele tower with mullioned windows.

Dalston, on the B5299 just south of Carlisle, is a pleasant village, but its chief glory is Dalston Hall, to the north, which like so many mansions in Cumbria is built round an old pele tower. The oldest parts have interesting carvings and inscriptions and, as at Burgh church, there is an iron "yatt".

Newbiggin Hall, just off the A6, is another old pele; once home of the priors of Carlisle.

At Wreay, reached by minor road east of the A6, six miles south of Carlisle, the Italian-style church, which looks so strange in a little Cumbrian village, has a reason equally strange for being here. It is a monument to the love of one sister for another.

Katherine and Sarah Losh, who lived at nearby Woodside, were the daughters of a prosperous Newcastle industrialist. They were the closest of friends and, when Katherine died in 1835, Sarah decided to build the church as a memorial to her. The sisters had travelled together in Italy and it was to the architecture of that warm and pleasant land that Sarah turned as inspiration for her church. Step inside and you're in a church like no other in Cumbria. The altar is in a semi-circular apse lined with columns and archways. There is sculpture, carvings and rich detail everywhere. Katherine is buried in a mausoleum of huge stone blocks, inside is a marble statue of her reading. In front of the mausoleum is a copy of the Bewcastle Cross and also to be seen in the churchyard is a copy of St Pirran's Chapel, Cornwall.

Wreay is proof that places don't have to date back centuries, or have been the site of famous events, to possess that indefinable "atmosphere" that makes certain places special.

Wetheral is on the B6263, which links the A6 and A69 roads, and forms a well-used short-cut for travellers wanting to avoid Carlisle. They hurry through this pretty sandstone village little knowing what lies just off their route. Wetheral once had a Benedictine priory and the gatehouse to this and a few sections of walling can still be seen, just south of Holy Trinity church. In the church itself is a beautiful monument to Lady Maria Howard, made by the sculptor Joseph Nollekens at the end of the 18th century. It shows a young woman with a baby lying on the ground, while an older woman, said to represent religion, bends over her.

South of the priory, paths drop through woodland into the gorge of the River Eden, where there are caves, said to have been used by St Constantine. You can see a statue of the saint on the opposite bank of the river.

The church of St Leonard at Warwick, on the A69 near Warwick Bridge, has a Norman apse with narrow windows. From it can be seen the eye-catching skyline of Holme Eden Abbey: an imposing mock Tudor mansion built for one of Carlisle's cotton magnates.

A minor road running south from the A69 brings one to Corby Castle; one of Cumbria's stately homes, which looks across the Eden to Wetheral. Corby began life as a pele tower, but as times got more peaceful and its owners became more prosperous it gradually branched out until its original defensive function was forgotten. The influential Howard family have been extending and embellishing their home from the 16th century onwards and their gardens are open to the public.

Cumwhitton, a couple of miles up the road, has one of Cumbria's oldest churches. An Anglo-Saxon window can be seen in the aisle and there is Norman zig-zag work.

Brampton is a pleasing place of rose-red stone. There are many interesting buildings in the broad main street, which lies just south of the traffic-laden A69. The most eye-catching is the moot hall, built in 1817.

Take the A6071, Longtown road, out of town and then the minor road to the left after the big schoolbuildings. At the end of this, on the site of a Roman fort and overlooking the meadows by the River Irthing, are the remains of Brampton old church, part of which dates back to Norman times.

On the east side of Brampton is an enormous mound, the motte of an old castle. It is surmounted by a statue of the 7th Earl of Carlisle. Brampton Junction Station is reached by a minor road from the A689 and lies to the south-east of the town. Thomas Edmondson was the first master at this curiously impressive station and he made his mark by inventing the ticket printing machine and introducing the familiar cardboard rail ticket. One of the first trains to stop here was the famous "Rocket".

Two miles east of Brampton, on the A69, a narrow road leads off left to drop through parkland until Naworth Castle, seeming to combine elegance with impregnability, comes into sight. From Naworth the Dacres and then the Howard family kept a watchful eye on the Scots across the debatable land to the north. It was built around a central courtyard in the 14th century and, although it suffered damage from fire last century, it was well restored. It is the home of the Earls of Carlisle.

If the lane is followed downhill it joins a larger road near a typically featureless modern bridge. But look to your right, where one of Cumbria's finest bridges shows that function and fine architecture can be combined. It was across this two-arched medieval bridge that black robed Augustinian canons journeyed to nearby Lanercost Priory.

This sandstone priory, part of which remains in use as a church, nestles beneath towering sycamores amid the watermeadows of the Irthing. The first view you have of it is framed in the archway of the ancient gatehouse. A small road crosses the field, flanked on the right by the vicarage and priory outbuildings. Ahead rises the west front of the priory: one of the finest sights in England. The priory ruins, and these are substantial, are tended by the Department of the Environment. There are vaulted roofs, ornate columns and monuments of the families of Naworth.

The church, which can be visited freely – though it would be a heartless person who didn't contribute to its upkeep – is half of the priory's chancel. Its east wall is a dividing wall put up after the Dissolution. High up on one of the walls is a Roman altar to Jupiter. It's a fair bet the builders didn't realise this when they were taking stones from the Roman wall to build with.

Lanercost was founded in 1166. Over the years it suffered damage in border raids. It also entertained that great enemy of the Scots, King Edward I.

To the east, and just off the A69, is Low Row, where a track can be followed to Denton Hall: an old farm with the remains of an even older pele tower. On the field in front is the motte of some Norman castle.

At Upper Denton, the next village, you can visit what must be one of England's oldest places of worship, built by the Anglo-Saxons, using stone from the Roman wall, and even incorporating a complete Roman arch in its chancel.

Just along the road is Gilsland and, though the bulk of the village is in Northumberland, the church is in Cumbria. Inside are two Roman altars. It was at Gilsland that the novelist Sir Walter Scott met his future wife Charlotte Carpenter. He proposed to her at a nearby beauty spot, known as the "Popping Stones".

A couple of miles along the B6318, Langholm road, another place with Scott connections can be seen. The surviving section of Triermain Castle stands gaunt and tall. It was the setting for Scott's poem "The Bridal of Triermain".

About three miles further on turn right for Bewcastle, but before this remote and historic spot is reached pause to look at Askerton Castle on the left hand side of the ride. Askerton is a 15th century manor house, fortified by the addition of towers at each side. These were built by Lord Dacre. The lawn and shrubs give Askerton the perfect setting.

Bewcastle nestles in the midst of glowering fells. Just the church, a ruined castle, a pub and a few homesteads are to be seen as you cross Kirk Beck to the green mound on the other bank. But here, in a spot that still looks wild in these peaceful days, is one of the wonders of English civilisation. In the year 670, Europe was still in the very darkest part of the so-called Dark Ages, yet, in the Anglian Kingdom of Northumbria, there had suddenly sprung up men of learning: poets, writers, illuminated manuscript illustrators and people who could carve stone with a poetic grace that has seldom been equalled before or since. Possibly their finest achievement is here: the stump of a once-mighty cross. Yet that stump still towers to more than 14 ft and on each face are carvings. A runic inscription says the cross commemorates "Alcfrith, once King son of Oswi". There are scenes from the Bible, of Christ and John the Baptist, and there is marvellously intricate scrollwork with animals and birds peering out from it.

Bewcastle itself stands on a Roman fort, the outline of which can still be seen and which has been the subject of recent excavations. Living in these bleak hills, on the Scottish side of Hadrian's Wall, must have been an unenvied billet among the legionaires.

North of Longtown is Kirkandrews. You're almost in Scotland here and you can feel it. Kirkandrews Tower was built by that famous border family the Grahams in the early 16th century and looks everyone's idea of a border raider's stronghold.

Half a mile further up the Esk are the remains of Liddel Strength, once one of the great castles of the Border country.

The name of Arthuret, just south of Longtown, has been used as backing by those who believe King Arthur lived and fought around Carlisle. Arthur's Seat, a hill to the east, might lend weight to their theory. There's a Norman cross in the churchyard and Arthuret church itself, built in the early 17th century, is beautifully proportioned. Inside a brass plaque showing two hands bearing a heart, indicates that a heart is buried here: a fairly common practice, especially if a body had perished before burial.

East of Longtown lies Brackenhill Tower, on the banks of the River Lyne. This was another Graham stronghold, being built in 1586. Further up the Lyne is Shank Castle, the ruined remnant of a pele tower with mullioned windows.

Scaleby Castle, south of the A6071, is another pele tower, converted by a series of additions into a fine house.

South-east of Houghton, near the M6, is Drawdykes Castle: a fine pele tower with a 17th century frontage built by John Aglionby. Further along the road is Linstock Castle; another pele, with a mullion-windowed range attached.

Linstock was once the home of the Bishops of Carlisle, who seem to have had a penchant for living away from their city. Edward I was a guest here on one of his border campaigns.

In the churchyard at Rockliffe, a small village to the east of the A74 and overlooking the Solway, is a cross decorated with dragons.

13   The Coal Towns

Between Whitehaven and Maryport the odds on meeting a tourist must be about the same as the odds on not meeting one at a place like Grasmere. For this part of Cumbria, with its mixture of corn fields and coal fields, chemical works and belching chimney stacks, is not to most people's taste. But put your prejudices behind you, for there is plenty of interest, as well as plenty that is undeniably unsightly.

For instance Whitehaven, would you believe it, was once England's third port, thriving on the coal trade to Ireland. In April, 1778, John Paul Jones, a local boy who had become an American citizen, landed as captain of the privateer Ranger to set fire to shipping here. Whitehaven had other trades and the 18th century Sugar Quay, which can still be visited, tells of one profitable line.

Whitehaven was laid out along classical lines by Christopher Wren, who drew up plans for Sir John Lowther. The old Lowther mansion, where this landowner lived, is now part of the town's hospital. St James's Church on Queen Street has a fine Georgian interior and a beautiful altar painting by Procaccini given by the Earl of Lonsdale and brought by him from Spain.

On Saltom Beach, to the south-west of the town, are the remains of Saltom Pit, built in 1731 to exploit coal reserves under the sea bed. Cleator Moor, a mining village on B5295, is dominated like many such places by its Co-Op. This one has a fine, ornate verandah. At Cleator, to the south, St Leonard's Church has a Norman window. On a minor road to the north-east of Whitehaven is beautiful Moresby Hall, built around 1690. It has a splendid Palladian front and was once the home of the Moresbys. Later the Fletchers lived here.

Just south of Distington, on the A595, just a wall remains of Hayes Castle.

Workington is a coal and iron town and generally of a grimness to match these heaviest of heavy industries. But Portland Square is a delightful oasis of charming houses laid out in the 18th century. There is also Workington Hall, built in 1379 with wings added in Elizabethan times. It was once home to the noted Curwen family and

Mary Queen of Scots spent her first night in England here, on the sad journey that was eventually to lead to her execution at Fotheringay Castle, Northamptonshire.

St Michael's Church, Workington, has some interesting old monuments and part of an Anglo-Saxon cross.

At Camerton, reached by minor road to the north-east, the church holds an effigy of Black Tom Curwen, dating from 1510. This redoubtable warrior clasps a great, double-handed sword.

Maryport gets its name from Mary, wife of Humphrey Senhouse, the lord of the manor, who developed it as a coal port in 1748. Nowadays it wears a rather depressed air, but there is plenty of character around the quayside. A house on the High Street has a plaque to record its distinction as the home of Isabella Harris, mother of Joseph Lister, of antiseptic fame. Netherhall, just outside the town, was the home of the Senhouses.

To the east, just off the A594, is Dearham, where the church, built around 1300, has part of a Viking cross inside its doorway, a carved Norman font and the Adam Stone, showing Christ with Adam and Eve.

To the north, off the A596, is Crosscannonby, where the church of St John the Evangelist has a hogback grave and is built partly of stones from a Roman fort. There is a carved gallery of 1730 and even older carved pews.

At Hayton, south-west of Aspatria, is Hayton Castle; a great rectangular building incorporating many architectural styles from the 15th century onwards.

In Aspatria itself the church, approached through a line of yews, has a Norman doorway, a Viking hogback grave, a Norman font and remains of crosses. The painted side chapel is dedicated to the Musgrave family.

14 On the Trail of Wordsworth and the Lake Poets

When the 18th century traveller had to journey through the Lake District, he did so with his head down, eyes on the way in front and making the best speed possible. He wasn't much interested in the lakes and mountains were fearful places one got away from as quickly as possible while the idea that anyone would want to paint or write poems about them would have seemed ridiculous.

But, as European civilisation became more complex and the coming of the machine age meant mankind and nature were drawing further apart, enlightened minds began to see the beauty of wild places and wild creatures, to appreciate banks of wild daffodils rather than formal gardens.

The Lake District, where every view seems to strive for perfection, might have been made for these people. Through their writings and paintings ordinary folk began to see the beauty too.

Perhaps the man who did most to popularise the Lake country was William Wordsworth, born at Cockermouth, in sight of the mountains, in 1770. He was the second son of five children born to John Wordsworth and his wife. The family home, an imposing Georgian building, stands at the end of Cockermouth main street. It is owned by the National Trust and visitors can see many Wordsworth relics here, or, shutting their ears to the noise of the passing traffic, imagine the poet's childhood days in this delightful house.

It's also worth saying a prayer of thanks that the age of enlightenment had gained just sufficient strength to save this building being demolished to make way for a bus station. The house was built in 1745 for the Sheriff of Cumberland. It was the property of Sir James Lowther, later Earl of Lonsdale, and John Wordsworth was agent to Sir James, looking after his extensive property in the area.

Wordsworth was baptised on the same day as his younger sister Dorothy. It was almost as if this was a symbol of how close the two were to remain. The young Wordsworths grew up in a house where education was valued. Their father had a good library and the children were expected to learn tracts of poetry by heart. Wordsworth went to Cockermouth Grammar School for a while. It stands close by the church.

But he and his family were not to know happiness for very long. Their mother Ann died in 1778 and five years later their father died too. His grave can be seen in All Saints Church, Cockermouth.

After his mother died, Wordsworth spent much time with his grandparents at Penrith and, while there, attended the local dame school. An attractive old building by the churchyard, built by Roger Bertram in 1563 and now housing a cafe, is said to have been where the school was held. A pupil here was Mary Hutchinson, who was to become Wordsworth's wife. Wordsworth stayed with his Cookson grandparents at a house in Devonshire Street.

The next stop on the Wordsworth trail is Hawkshead where the old grammar school, with its round chimney stacks and roughcast walls, was attended by William. The walls now bear Wordsworth quotations and Wordsworth's signature, on his desk, is lovingly protected by glass. If it had been spotted at the time it's more likely he would have been branded a "young ruffian" and cuffed soundly!

Wordsworth came to Hawkshead in 1779 and, with his brother, lodged at the cottage of joiner Hugh Tyson and wife Ann. Their cottage may or may not have been the one pointed out at Grandy Nook. Some folk say the Tysons lived at nearby Colthouse.

From Hawkshead Wordsworth went out into the world; to Cambridge, where he read poetry, and to France, where he had a passionate affair and later espoused the principles of the French Revolution. But his Lakeland upbringing drew him back.

In 1794 he was offered accommodation at Keswick, where he befriended the ailing son of the family and was rewarded in the latter's will. This legacy gave him the means to buy a property of his own. In December, 1799, he and Dorothy set up home in Town End, a small cottage at Grasmere that had once been known as the Dove and Olive Bough inn. Today, as Dove Cottage, this homely building is known the world over. Furnished as in the Wordsworths' time it is kept as a shrine to the poet: a barn over the road is the Wordsworth Museum. In these irreligious days writers seem to have replaced saints as subjects of veneration!

Around 1800 there may have been less visitors, but their names read like a "Who's Who" of English literature. A frequent visitor was Samuel Taylor Coleridge, who had lived with them in the south of England and moved to Greta Hall, Keswick, in 1800. This house, which later became the home of Poet Laureate Robert Southey, is now a boarding school. The grave of Southey, who died in 1843, can be seen on the north side of nearby Crosthwaite Church.

Another frequent visitor at Dove Cottage was Thomas De Quincey, best remembered for his book "Confessions of an Opium Eater". He lived with the Wordsworths for a time and later at Nab Cottage, which stands near the shore of Rydal Water on the road between Grasmere and Rydal and is now a guest house.

One visitor was Sir Walter Scott who is said to have found the meal offered him rather meagre and to have sneaked out of a window to get second helpings at a local inn.

Although Wordsworth didn't spend a great part of his life at Dove Cottage, it was the years he spent here which produced much of his best work. De Quincey moved into Dove Cottage in 1808 when Wordsworth, by now married and a proud parent, moved into grandiose Allan Bank, which he rented from a Liverpool merchant. Allan Bank, reached from Grasmere village square, is a private home but it can be seen from the surrounding parkland. Ironically Wordsworth had once condemned this house as an "abomination" on the landscape. He was now beginning to make his way in the world and the revolutionary ideals of youth were being replaced by an equally ardent belief in "the Establishment".

In 1811 the Wordsworths moved into Grasmere Rectory, as the rector was living elsewhere. The Rectory, which has been much rebuilt, stands opposite the village church. It was not a happy home for the family who saw two children die here.

Meanwhile, Lord Lonsdale, the family patron, obtained for Wordsworth the commission to sell stamps in Westmorland: a position which brought him a comfortable £300 a year. The family's next home was more in keeping with their new status. Rydal Mount, just down the valley at Rydal, is an impressive building which the family rented from an absentee landlady. But there was sadness here too, for Dorothy became mentally ill.

In 1843 Wordsworth became Poet Laureate. He died on April 23rd, 1850, with his ideas and ideals now shared by millions. Dorothy died five years later and his wife Mary in 1859. Their graves, and those of two of the Wordsworth children, can be seen at St Oswald's Church, Grasmere. Living reminders of the poet are the churchyard yews which Wordsworth helped to plant and to pay for.

Near Patterdale, at the head of Ullswater, is Broad How, where William and Dorothy stayed for a time and where they had plans to build a home. At Gowbarrow Park, just down the lake, can be seen the daffodils which Wordsworth saw in April, 1802, and which inspired his most famous poem.

BEATRIX POTTER

Beatrix Potter was another writer who loved the Lakes; weaving her marvellous tapestry of children's stories on threads drawn from Lakeland life and character. She was born in 1866 and spent her earliest years in London, so, when her family rented Wray Castle, a Victorian folly at Sawrey now used to train seamen, a whole new world was opened up to her. It was the sort of world she had only imagined in childhood fantasies and written about in her "Tale of Peter Rabbit".

With the royalties from this book Beatrix was able to buy Hill Top Farm at Sawrey and here she came to stay, writing her books and doing the delightful water colour illustrations at which she was equally adept. In 1913, at the age of 47, she married solicitor William Heelis and the couple moved to Castle Cottage, just a few hundred yards away.

Hill Top remained a sort of private sanctuary for Beatrix, who had added the talents of a sheep breeder to those of writer and illustrator. She became a passionate campaigner for Lakeland preservation and, on her death in 1943, left Hill Top to the National Trust. Now it can be visited and you can see her notebook, furnishings and doll collection preserved as they were in her day.

JOHN RUSKIN

Ruskin, the great art critic, writer and campaigner for Lakeland preservation, lived at Brantwood on the east shore of Coniston Water. Brantwood is open to visitors who can see works by Turner and other leading artists.

In Coniston village is a small museum about Ruskin and other topics of local interest. In Coniston churchyard a handsome memorial stands above his grave.

HORACE WALPOLE

Horace Walpole lived at Brackenburn, a house on the slopes of that most attractively-named of Lakeland hills, Catbells, just a couple of miles south-west of Keswick and overlooking Derwentwater. He built the house in 1923 and died here in 1941. He based his series of novels "The Herries Chronicles", on Lakeland life. Some of Walpole's possessions can be seen in the museum at Keswick and the writer is buried at the south-west corner of St John's Church, Keswick.

GEORGE ROMNEY

George Romney, one of the greatest of English portrait painters, was a Cumbrian. He was born at Dalton-in-Furness in 1734, the son of a farmer-cum-builder, and as a lad was apprenticed to a joiner; much to his displeasure. Romney was later reapprenticed to a painter at Redman's Yard, Kendal, where a plaque commemorates this.

At this time Romney was ill and the young girl who nursed him back to health later became his wife. Her care for the painter was not reciprocated, for Romney left her with two young children to find fame and fortune in London, where he painted such notables as Emma, Lady Hamilton. He later returned to his family and died at Kendal in 1802. In Kendal church is a black marble monument to him. His grave can be seen in the churchyard at Dalton-in-Furness.

THE MAN WHO SAVED THE LAKES.

Canon Hardwick Drummond Rawnsley could be called the man who saved the Lake District . . . from over-exploitation. A follower of Ruskin, Rawnsley was vicar of Crosthwaite Church, Keswick, from 1883 to 1917. He was the moving spirit of the foundation of the National Trust. which now preserves so many Lakeland acres and historic buildings.

Rawnsley is buried at Crosthwaite and there are memorials to him and Ruskin on the path to that famous Derwentwater beauty spot Friars Crag.

LADY ANNE.

Wherever you turn in eastern Cumbria you seem to come across the influence of Lady Anne Clifford, later Countess of Pembroke, who left her.mark so deeply on this land.

She was born in 1590 and, following the death of her father and a legal tussle with her uncle, bcame the owner of vast estates. An unhappy marriage seemed to draw Anne closer to her mother and, in spite of the bad roads of that age, she would often travel north to see her parent at Brougham Castle, south of Penrith.

Anne was summoned to return by her husband, and mother and daughter had a sad parting a short way down the road from the castle. Shortly after her mother died. Now, at the side of the busy A66, Countess's Pillar tells the moving story of that parting. Margaret, Anne's mother, is buried at St Lawrence's Church,

Appleby, where Anne built a suitably impressive tomb. In time Lady Anne was to be buried here herself.

Anne and her husband were reconciled before his death. After this she married Philip Herbert and became Countess of Pembroke. Many Clifford properties suffered during the Civil War; with peace and the death of her second husband, Lady Anne devoted her considerable energy and resources to restoring them and building new ones.

In Appleby there are almshouses built in memory of her mother in 1651. The castle, built in the 11th century, was restored by her, as were Brough, Brougham and Pendragon castles. Many churches were also restored.

It was one of Anne's customs to present her tenants with initialled padlocks and locks bearing the letters "A.P.", for Anne, Countess of Pembroke, can be seen at Collingfield House, Kendal and at Dacre church.

15   Hadrian's Wall

Cumbria is fortunate in having a portion of what is probably the world's greatest Roman monument: Hadrian's Wall. This famous frontier fortification was built around A.D. 122 by the Roman governor of Britain, Aulus Platorius Nero after the Emperor Hadrian had come in person to Britain to see what could be done to avenge the Ninth Legion, which had been destroyed in Scotland, and to make sure that an increasingly peaceful and prosperous England was kept safe from the fierce northern tribesmen.

For long periods the wall was not, as many people imagine, the front-line defence. In fact it was the opposite: for Roman legions controlled much of Scotland. But should they be destroyed or swept aside by new risings the wall would be there to fall back on and prevent incursions into England.

The wall, more than 70 miles long, ran between Wallsend-on-Tyne and Bowness-on-Solway. Defences continued along the Cumbrian coast with forts to prevent seaborne invasions. Along the wall itself milecastles, holding a couple of dozen troops, were built every Roman mile; between each of these were two turrets. In addition there were 17 forts where up to 1,000 men were stationed.

The section of the wall between Irthing and the Solway was originally made of turf and only later built of stone. To the south of the wall was built the vallum, a steep-sided trench which may have acted as a secondary barrier or, perhaps, prevented attack from the rear. In spite of all these precautions the wall was overthrown on three occasions. But each time is was reoccupied and rebuilt, until the Romans finally left Britain in the 4th century.

Gilsland is the centre for exploring the best sections of Roman Wall in Cumbria. In the vicarage garden, to the west of the rail line, still stands 220 yards of wall. Notice the broad foundations on which sits a much narrower wall, indicating that the Romans never got round to building this section of their defences as strongly as they had planned. Access is from the Gilsland–Low Row road, between the vicarage and the school.

To the south of the rail line, reached by a path from the station, is the Poltross Burn Milecastle.

About 1,000 yards of wall, in fact the best section in Cumbria, can be seen running west of the Low Row road to the River Irthing. It includes two turrets and, at the river, the remains of the Willowford bridge abutment, where the wall crossed the Irthing and where the Romans had a water mill. One of the original bridge piers can still be seen.

On the other bank of the river, but reached by car along the B6318 north from Gilsland and turning left down a minor road, is Birdoswald and the Roman fort of Camboglanna. There is a good section of Roman wall here as well as the remains of the five-acre fort, of which the south and east gateways and fort walls are particularly well preserved.

Just along the road from Birdoswald is the Harrows Scar mile-castle, where the turf wall used to begin. Continuing along this road, which can also be reached from Brampton, the Piper Syke Turret and Leahill Turret are to be seen. Further along still, at Banks, is a very well preserved turret and stretch of wall 10 ft high. There is a memorial to a Roman centurion in its base.

At Walton, reached by minor road to the right of the A6071 Brampton–Longtown road, can be seen a turret and a small stretch of wall in a field to the west of Dovecote Bridge, where it spans the Kings Water. To the west of Carlisle, at Drumburgh, between Burgh and Bowness, a small stretch of wall remains. There are Roman memorials at Bowness.